W. F. Chapman

Wildair's birthday party

W. F. Chapman

Wildair's birthday party

ISBN/EAN: 9783337818265

Printed in Europe, USA, Canada, Australia, Japan

Cover: Foto ©ninafisch / pixelio.de

More available books at **www.hansebooks.com**

WILDAIR'S BIRTHDAY PARTY.

CHARACTERS :

Mr. Peter Poddles (Wildair's Uncle).

Will Wildair (Studying for the Bar).

Harry Hallwit (" A fellow of infinite jest ").

Septimus Smyler (who cannot help smiling).

Antonio Agrippa (a would-be tragedian).

Mrs. Moppy (proprietress of a boarding-house. For further particulars enqure within).

Moses (her servant).

Explanation of the capitals :—R, right ; C, centre ; L, left. The performer is supposed to face the audience.

Scene—Wildair's *room in* Mrs. Moppy's *establishment; chairs, table, C; small table L; large chest, R.*

[*Enter* Moses, *carrying decanters (containing liquid to imitate wine) and glasses on tray.*]

It says in the copy-book " Wine is a mocker," and I think it is too ; so I'll put the " mocker " on the table (*puts tray on table, L*), and improve my mind with a little modern literatoore. (*Produces book from beneath his vest*). This is where I keeps my liberiary. I often always like sometimes occasionally to read these books of adventoore; but the old woman doesn't allow me to read them, so I have to keep them dark, then she thinks I don't read them, but don't I,—oh rawther. (*Opens book*). This is the most thrilling tale I ever saw. It's called " The Plunderin' Pirates' Perfidy ; or the Ragman's Rewenge." Now let me see, where was I ?—oh ere's the place. (*Reads.*) The valiant captain, headed by his unfaithful crew, rushed upon the deck to welcome the marauders. A terrific hand-to-hand conflict ensued ! The fight was ragin' furiously, when a sweet and soft voice from the mast-head, at the bow, near the stern, called out in stentorian tones——

Mrs. YOPPY
MOSES.—Oh   ne.
(*Tries to hide ι*   ιs,
takes a large ι   .ES
round and roun   ng
the while). ᷄
Mrs. M.—Al   in'
that book ag'in   ι [
can see it behi   'll
give yer a taste
MOSES.—I'd   ry
well without it
Mrs. M.—W   ιts
to strike MOSES   *lis*
book on the tabl   rs.
Mrs. Moppy *jι*   *ns*
out. She does   *m,*
sawing the air ι   *it*
with the stick).
Mrs. M.—Tl   ·d,
would yer?]   ad
them vile book
        (WILL ᷄
WILD.—Hal   r?
(*Puts his hat o.*
Mrs. M.— Chair! (*Pushes it away*). Oh, er—I was, er—I was
ח dustin' the chair, sir. (*Appears exhausted, sits.*)
WILD.—*Dusting* the chair, were you? Oh, I see, a patent
ᴨrocess. It seems easier than rubbing with a cloth; much easier.
ι suppose the stick is used to get in the corners.
Mrs. M.—Well, the fac' is I wasn't dustin' That boy Moses 'as
ᴨ*rag'erated* me, an'——
WILD.—Exasperated, I suppose you mean.
Mrs. M.—I *said* exag'erated. An' when you saw me a wollopin'
ιhe chair I thought I was a wallopin' 'im. Oh, deary me; it's
made quite fati-gued an' set my 'art all on a *parapet*.
WILD.—Palpitate, not parapet, Mrs. Moppy. Your vocabulary
seems to be somewhat disordered.
Mrs. M.—Oh, no, Mr. Wildair. I never was troubled with that
complaint, as yet; hit ain't my *vocality* what's disordered, I'm
afeard I'm a goin' to 'ave a attack o' the *spagms*, I does. Oh, my !
WILD.—Now don't go on in that way, Mrs. Moppy. I expect

my friends here every moment. As I told you yesterday, I want the dinner to be a perfect triumph of culinary art. Wo dine at five; don't forget; five prompt.

Mrs. M.—Very well, Mr. Wildair, it shall be ready on the himpulso of the *monument*. (*Rises*).

WILD.—Moment, Mrs. Moppy, moment.

Mrs. M.—I *said* monument! Ah, well, I'll go. (*Goes to door*.) I 'opes as yer'll enjoy yerselves to-night, I does. (*Coming to front again*.) I frequent says, Mr. Wildair, as 'ow wo allus should enjoy hourselves on the *adversary* of our birthday—*devidin'* we feels that way dispoged, an' why shouldn't we ?

WILD.—I don't know of any reason why we should not, if as you say, we feel that way disposed. But you will see that there is nothing spoiled in the kitchen, Mrs Moppy ; hadn't you better go down and—

Mrs. M.—Mr. Wildair, I'll go himmegently. (*Goes to door*.)

WILD.—Very good, Mrs Moppy, very good. (*Sits*)

Mrs. M.—(*Coming to front*).—An' I allus remarks, Mr. Wildair—

WILD. (*rises*).—What, again ; Now Mrs. Moppy, what——

Mrs. M.—I say I frequent remarks that what gives me the mostist *sausagefatshun* at a birthday party is to-hear the guest a wishin' the birthdayist the many arppy *reforms* o' the day. I wishes yer a many hoffen 'arppy *reforms* o' this day, I does, Mr. Wildair, an' I opes that at some not wery *distinct* time yer'll be wery rich an' rize to 'igher *spears* : be *a* Dook, or *a* Markis, or *a* Nearl; an' ride about in yer wery own *barookay* among all the *aristoescratic* people o' the land ; or, if yer gets on in yer *confession* as *a* lawyer, an' gets 'eavy damages for a forsookt young lady in a breek o' promige ca:e ,I 'opes as yer'll like the young lady an' take her for your own *awful* wife—an', in course, the 'eavy damages likewige.

WILD.—This is all very well, Mrs. Moppy, but really now, between ourselves, don't you think that you had better bring your dissertatious to a close, and depart at once to the abode of cookery? (*Sits*).

Mrs. M.—I'll go this *instinct !* Well, I wishes' yer many 'arppy *reforms*; many 'arppy *reforms*. Now, I'm goin'. I say, I'm goin'.

WILD.—Very well! Don't *say* you are going, but *go !*

Mrs. M.—Mr. Wildair, I am imvidgible ! (*Exit*.)

WILD.—And it is quite time you were. When once Mrs. Moppy's tongue is set in motion her fluency of speech is positively amazing, for she never knows when to stop. It's awfully jolly to have your pals to dinner; far more enjoyable than studying for the Bar.

Mrs. Yoppy (*calling without*).—Moses! Moses!

Moses.—Oh, my eye! That's the misses a callin' after me. (*Tries to hide the book behind him. Enter Mrs. Moppy, sees Moses, takes a large walking stick from the corner. She follows Moses round and round the table, brandishing the walking stick and speaking the while*).

Mrs. M.—Ah; so yer 'ere, are yer? I've catcht yer peroosin' that book ag'in, 'ave I? Oh, it ain't no use tryin' to hide it, 'cos I can see it behind yer. Come 'ere, yer young jacknapes, an I'll give yer a taste o' this stick.

Moses.—I'd rawther be excused, Mrs. Moppy. I can do very well without it—oh, rawther.

Mrs. M.—We'll see whether you can do without it. (*Attempts to strike Moses with the stick. He runs round the room, throws his book on the table, L; crawls under table, C; dodges round the chairs. Mrs. Moppy follows, making wild attempts to strike him. He runs out. She does not see him go, but continues running about the room, sawing the air with the walking stick, then seizes a chair and beats it with the stick*).

Mrs. M.—There—there—there.! You'd rather be hexcused, would yer? Yer can do without the stick, can yer? Yer'll read them vile books, again, will yer?

(Will Wildair *stands in the doorway, watching her.*)

Wild.—Hallo! Mrs Moppy, what are you doing to the chair? (*Puts his hat on table, L*).

Mrs. M.—Chair! (*Pushes it away*). Oh, er—I was, er—I was a dustin' the chair, sir. (*Appears exhausted, sits.*)

Wild.—*Dusting* the chair, were you? Oh, I see, a patent process. It seems easier than rubbing with a cloth; much easier. I suppose the stick is used to get in the corners.

Mrs. M.—Well, the fac' is I wasn't dustin' That boy Moses 'as exag'erated me, an'——

Wild.—Exasperated, I suppose you mean.

Mrs. M.—I *said* exag'erated. An' when you saw me a wollopin' the chair I thought I was a wallopin' 'im. Oh, deary me; it's made quite fati-gued an' set my 'art all on a *parapet*.

Wild.—Palpitate, not parapet, Mrs. Moppy. Your vocabulary seems to be somewhat disordered.

Mrs. M.—Oh, no, Mr. Wildair. I never was troubled with that complaint, as yet; hit ain't my *vocality* what's disordered, I'm afeared I'm a goin' to 'ave a attack o' the *spagms*, I does. Oh, my!

Wild.—Now don't go on in that way, Mrs. Moppy. I expect

my friends here every monent. As I told you yesterday, I want
the dinner to be a perfect triumph of culinary art. We dine at
five ; don't forget ; five prompt.

Mrs. M.—Very well, Mr. Wildair, it shall be ready on the him-
pulse of the *monument.* (*Rises*).

WILD.—Moment, Mrs. Moppy, moment.

Mrs. M.—I *said* monument! Ah, well, I'll go. (*Goes to door.*)
I 'opes as yer'll enjoy yerselves to-night, I does. (*Coming to front
again.*) I frequent says, Mr. Wildair, as 'ow we allus should
enjoy hourselves on the *adversary* of our birthday—*devidin'* we
feels that way dispoged, an' why shouldn't we ?

WILD.—I don't know of any reason why we should not, if as you
say, we feel that way disposed. But you will see that there is
nothing spoiled in the kitchen, Mrs Moppy ; hadn't you better go
down and—

Mrs. M.—Mr. Wildair, I'll go himmegently. (*Goes to door.*)

WILD.—Very good, Mrs Moppy, very good. (*Sits*)

Mrs. M.—(*Coming to front*).—An' I allus remarks, Mr. Wildair—

WILD. (*rises*).—What, again ; Now Mrs. Moppy, what——

Mrs. M.—I say I frequent remarks that what gives me the mostist
sausagefatshun at a birthday party is to-hear the guest a wishin'
the birthdayist the many arppy *reforms* o' the day. I wishes yer
a many hoffen 'arppy *reforms* o' this day, I does, Mr. Wildair, an'
I opes that at some not wery *distinct* time yer'll be wery rich an'
rize to 'igher *spears* : be *a* Dook, or *a* Markis, or *a* Nearl ; an' ride
about in yer wery own *barookay* among all the *aristoescratic* people
o' the land ; or, if yer gets on in yer *confession* as *a* lawyer, an'
gets 'eavy damages for a forsookt young lady in a breek o' promige
case ,I 'opes as yer'll like the young lady an' take her for your own
awful wife—an', in course, the 'eavy damages likewige.

WILD.—This is all very well, Mrs. Moppy, but really now,
between ourselves, don't you think that you had better bring your
dissertations to a close, and depart at once to the abode of cookery?
(*Sits*).

Mrs. M.—I'll go this *instinct !* Well, I wishes' yer many 'arppy
reforms ; many 'arppy *reforms.* Now, I'm goin'. I say, I'm goin'.

WILD.—Very well ! Don't *say* you are going, but *go !*

Mrs. M.—Mr. Wildair, I am imvidgible ! (*Exit.*)

WILD.—And it is quite time you were. When once Mrs. Moppy's
tongue is set in motion her fluency of speech is positively amazing,
for she never knows when to stop. It's awfully jolly to have
your pals to dinner ; far more enjoyable than studying for the Bar.

I hate study! In fact I abhor anything that resembles work. It's not because I am lazy—oh, dear no—but I would rather be busy doing a great deal of nothing: much rather; unfortunately, I have not my own course to choose. I was left an orphan at a very early age, and was taken in tow by my uncle Peter, who very kindly promised to pilot me through the dangers of this busy world. I concurred with my uncle Peter in everything he said; declared that I was delighted with the *cheerful* prospect, and expressed my willingness to depart to town immediately, if he wished. Uncle Peter did not wish for my *immediate* departure, however, but said I should go the following week. The following week arrived, and so did I—in town; took apartments in " Mrs. Moppy's boarding establishment for single gentlemen," and commenced studying slowly—very slowly; in fact so slowly that I know as much about law as—as Mrs. Moppy knows about the dictionary! Of course my good old Uncle Peter thinks I am advancing wonderfully in my studies, and frequently says in his letters that he will come and see how I am getting on as soon as he has an opportunity. Now I sincerely hope and trust that the opportunity will not present itself for a considerable period. Some time in the dim future I *may* be glad to welcome him to these halls; but a visit from him at present would be far—very far from gratifying." (*Knock at Door.*) Come in!

MOSES (*enters*).—A couple of gentlemen—two in number—want to sees you, sir. They say their names are Mr. Septimus Smyler and Mr. Larry Hall Wittles. Ah! they are coming in now without asking.

(*Enter* SMYLER and HALLWIT.)

MOSES (*aside*).—That's what I call ignorance. Don't they think they are swell?—oh, rawther!

HALL (*Shaking Wildair's hand*).—How are you, old fellow? you see we've taken the liberty to walk in without waiting the return of this energetic retainer of yours. I hope I see you well. In fact I hope you will never be visible in any other state of health; and, as this is the *first* time you have reached your twenty-second birthday, I have very great pleasure in wishing you innumberable felicitous repetitions of the day—very great pleasure.

WILD.—For all these kind wishes accept my most sincere thanks. Moses, show Mr. Agrippa in as soon as he arrives.

MOSES.—I can't very conveniently show him in *before* he arrives, sir!

WILD.—Get out! you young dog. (*Exit* MOSES).

5

SEP. (*Shaking Wildair's hand*)—How d you do, Will; how d'you do?

HALL.—The best he can of course.

SEP.—Ha, ha, ha! Yes to be sure. I say, Will, I—I was just about to say what our friend Harry has said, but unfortunately he had exactly the same idea. You don't care about hearing it repeated, do you?

WILD.—Oh dear no; *not at all*, Septimus.

HALL.—What's that? *Not a tall Septimus!* Well, he's rather *tall* for his *height*.

SEP.—Ha, ha, ha! Good joke--very good.

WILD.—Oh I say Harry, don't stand there joking; please to take a chair.

HALL.—With pleasure; I'll take them all if you wish.

SEP.—Ha, ha, ha!—very sharp. I—I was just about to make the same remark.

HALL.—You don't say so.

(*Knock at door.* HALLWIT *and* SEPTIMUS *sit.*)

(*Enter* MOSES, *followed by* ANTONIO AGRIPPA.)

MOSES.—Mr. Antonynose Adrip tinpot has arrived, sir, (*Aside.*) Ain't that a name?—oh, rawther.

WILD (*to* MOSES).—Antonio Agrippa you mean. Leave the room- (*Exit* MOSES.)

ANTONIO (*to* WILDAIR).—Do not chide the youth. William Shake speare says—

What's in a name? that which we call a rose
By any other name would smell as sweet.

How is it with you?—(*Shaking hands with* WILDAIR)—I wish you many happy returns of this your birthday.

WILD.—Thank you Antonio.

SEP. (*Rises; shakes* AGRIPPA'S *hand*).—How d'you do, Antonio? How d'you do?

ANT.—I am well, I thank you, Septimus. I did not *see* you sitting there.

SEP.—Didn't you, though? My friends tell me I am going very thin. Some go so far as to say that I am in a *consumption*, but I—er——

HALL.—You *decline* to believe it?

SEP.—Ha, ha, ha! Yes. Consumption—decline. I see it.

ANT. (*Sees* HALLWIT).—What; do I *behold* young Harry? (*Seizes* HALLWIT'S *hand; shakes it warmly.* HALLWITT *rises*).

HALL.—Oh! I say! You might *be hold*-ing *Old* HARRY by the way you squeeze my hand. (*Examines his fingers*). By Jove! you are *Agrippa* (a gripper).

SEP.—Ha, ha, ha! Agrippa; yes, of course! I—I was just going to make the same joke myself.

WILD.—I say, Harry, I wish you would have the goodness NOT to make those *puns*.

HALL.—*Upun* my word, I can't help it.

SEP.—Ha, ha; there's another.

ANT.—And how is it with you, Harry? Art well?

HALL.—Moderately so, Mr. A.; how may you B! I hope I C you well; in D'd you look well; don't E, Will? I don't think I Fer saw him looking better.

SEP.—Ha, ha, ha! Cleverly arranged. *A., b., c., d., e., f*—capital—capital.

HALL.—Yes they are *capital* letters, arn't they?

ANT.—To quote the immortal William's words, thou'rt " a follow of infinite jest," Harry.

SEP.—I—I, was going to make a first rate joke when you said Mr. A. but you put me out through following on so quickly with the other letters.

HALL.—Indeed, *letters* (let us) hear it.

SEP.—When you said Mr. A., I was going to say *straw*.

HALL.—Ex-*straw*-dinary! But where's the joke?

SEP.—Don't you see it?—*Hay—Straw*.

HALL.—Eh! (*shakes his head*) no; you must be *chaff*-ing.

WILD.—Oh hang it, Harry, I wish you would have the goodness *not* to make those jokes; sit down. Antonio, Septimus, take your seats, please. (HALLWIT, SEPTIMUS, *and* ANTONIO *sit round the table C.*)

ANT.—By-the-bye, ████, I have written an *Ode*, consisting of five hundred lines, in honour of your birthday. (*Produces a large roll of paper.*) I will read them for you. (*Rises, unrolls the paper.*) You remember the ode I composed in honour of Charles Hepper's birthday?

WILD. (*is removing the decanters and glasses to table C*).—Yes. I remember it well, (*aside*) too well, I don't want to hear another like it. (*Aloud*). I am sure you are very kind, Antonio, in putting yourself to so much trouble on my account; but er—you shall have an opportunity to read your Ode presently.

SEP.—Yes; we'll hear it in a while.

HALL.—Certainly, in a while; not now. (*Aside*). It doesn't do to hurry these *od(e)*ious things.

Ant.—Very well ; as you please. But why let the present opportunity pass ? (*The others applaud him and say*—" *Bravo ! Hear, hear ! Very good."*) Shall I read my ode now ?

Wild.—Not at present, Antonio, if you please.

Ant.—Be't so. (*Sits*).

Wild.— You will take a glass of *wine*, Septimus, and you, Harry ? (*Fills four glasses.*)

Hall.—Of course, *wine hot*, (why not ?)

Sep.—Ha, ha, ha ! Why not—wine hot. Good ! I—I was just going to make the same joke myself.

Wild.—Punning again. I *do* wish you would leave off that *old habit*, Harry.

Hall.—Now I think this *habit suits* me very well (indicating his clothes). *Old* habit, indeed ! Why it is nearly new, and I can't afford to leave it off yet. You know we poor fellows don't *Walkin' tour suits* (walk into our suits) as easily as you.

Sep.—Ha, ha, ha ! Bravo—good joke.

Wild.—I wish you would have the goodness not to make jokes, Harry ; you are a complete bore.

Ant.—Ha, ha, ha ! I cannot help laughing at his jokes. To quote the poet Shakespeare's words—

> " A merrier man
> Within the limits of becoming mirth
> I never spent an hour's talk withal."

Shall I read my *ode*, now ?

Hall.—O, *dear*, Antonio, wait a bit, please ?

Sep.—Ha, ha, ha !—good again.

Wild.—You must be troubled with the punning disease.

Hall.—I once knew a fellow who was afflicted in the same way ; he cracked jokes incessantly. Ultimately, he cracked a joke concerning the personal charms of a member of the fraternity know as prize-fighters. The pugilist reciprocated the compliment by cracking the punster's head ; and on the receipt of this kind mark of his appreciation the jocose individual immediately departed this life. Moral : if you do not want your heads cracked or otherwise tastefully ornamented, avoid joking.

Ant. (*Rises and unrolls paper*).—Now friends, shall I read my ode ?

Wild.—Presently, Antonio ; all in good time.

Ant.—Very well. As you please. (*Sits*).

Hall. (*rises*).—Gentlemen, let us drink to the health of our worthy host, and wish him, once more, many happy returns of the day.

Sep., Ant., Hall.—We wish you many happy returns of this day. (*They drink and sit.*)

Wild. (*rises*).—Friends of my bosom, at this moment, one of the proudest of my life,——

Hall.—Hear, hear!

Wild.—I find it is impossible to express in adequate terms my thanks for your kind wishes with regard to the length of my stay upon this terrestrial globe, and my feelings at this moment overwhelm me with emotion, as I reflect upon the earnestness with which you have on this occasion drunk my health, and—er—drunk my wine!

Ant.—Shall I read my ode, now? (*Rises, unrolls paper.*)

Wild.—Very good, Antonio. And then it will be time to take dinner.

Ant. (*Rises, unrolls paper—clears his voice and reads*).—Age, age, age, age, age, age, age, age, a——

Hall.—Pardon my interruption, but don't you think that sounds monotonous? May I enquire how many times the word age is repeated?

Ant.—Twenty-two! it is a concise way of stating the age of our friend, William. A brilliant idea, is it not?

Hall.—Very! pray proceed.

Ant. (*Reads*).—Age, age, age, a——

[*Enter* Moses *staggering under the weight of a large portmanteau he lets it fall to the floor. The others are startled, and rise from their seats.*]

Moses.—Phew! Ain't that heavy?—oh, rawther.

Wild. (*to* Moses).—Where the dickens have you got that from?

Moses.— A gentleman which came in a cab told me to take it to your room, sir, so I took it accordin'. He says the cabby has over-charged him, an' ain't he blowing him up?—oh, rawther.

Wild.—Who can it be? (*Reads label on the Portmanteau*). Peter Poddles, passenger to——ten thousands thunders! it's my uncle Peter. (*Walks about agitatedly*).

Hall.—What's the row, old fellow. Are you training for a six days' walking match?

Wild.—Don't you understand? It's my uncle Peter. (*Walks about agitatedly*).

Hall.—I don't care if it's saltpetre! We shall not object to his company.

Wild.—But if he sees you here I shall be lost.

HALL.—No you won't; we'll come in search of you.

WILD.—Oh, Harry, *do* be serious. My uncle will be up stairs in a minute or two, and if he sees you three here he will cut me off with a shilling.

HALL.—Never mind ; we'll help you to spend it.

WILD.—Moses, don't allow that gentleman to come upstairs Tell him that I am—er—busily engaged !—very busily engaged. (*Exit* MOSES.) Now, friends, what am I to do ?

ANT.—"Go you and greet him." Those words are Shakespeare's.

WILD.—Not I. *I* know him—*you* don't. The fact is my uncle must not know you are here. (*Points to the door*). That is the only way out of this room, and if you go that way he will see you coming out ; so what's to be done ; I don't see anything else for it but hiding you somewhere.

HALL.—All right ! I'll get inside the *portmanteau*.

WILD.—Don't be an ass.

HALL.—Any *port-man-teau* escape a storm.

WILD.—Here, Septimus, get under this table, quick ! (*Forces* SEPTIMUS *under table L*).

HALL.—What about the dinner, Will ?

WILD.—Oh, bother the dinner.

HALL.—*Dinna* forget, as the Scotchman said.

SEP. (*Raises the tablecloth and looks out*).—Ha, ha, ha ! Good joke.

WILD.—You get under this table, Harry. (*Rushes* HALLWIT *under table C*. *H. remonstrates*). Keep still and then you will be *comfortable*.

HALL. (*Raises tablecloth and looks out*).—I didn't 'com-for-table at all. I came for dinner.

WILD.—Where can I put you, Antonio ? Is there room under there, Harry ?

HALL.—No ; we're quite full inside.

ANT.—Where must I go ? "Oh that this too solid flesh would melt, thaw, and resolve itself into a dew," as Shakespeare observes.

WILD.—(*Looks round the room. Goes to chest*, R). Here, Antonio, you can get inside my lumber chest ! (*Opens chest*). Do be quick.

ANT. (*Gets in the Chest*).—You will release me as soon as you can ?

WILD.—Yes of course I will. (*Forces him down by the lid*. ANT. *raises the lid again*. WILD. *pushes it down. They repeat this business three or four times*. *When* WILD. *goes away* ANT. *looks out.*)

WILD. (*Sees glasses, &c*).—I must put these out of my uncle PETER's sight, or there *will* be a row. (*Noise without*. WILD. *puts the glasses and decanters in a corner, and places the portmanteau before them*).

MOSES (*without*).—It ain't no use, I tell you; you can't go inside that room, sir.

PODDLES (*without*).—Stand out of my way, will you.

WILD.—Here he is; what must I do? Ah here's a book. (*Takes Moses's book from the table L.*) Uncle Peter must find me studying. Now friends, keep strict silence, and all will be well.

HALL.—It's all very well taking about *preserving* silence while I'm in this *pickle jam*-med under a table.

SEP.—Ha, ha, ha! Preserve—jam—pickle—very good!

HALL.—What, the pickles?

SEP.—No, the joke.

WILD.—Be quiet, my uncle is coming. (*Noise without*. WILD. *sits*, R. *end of table, acts nervously, opens the book on the table*)

HALL.—All right; good night everybody. I'll draw the curtains and repose in my novel four-post bedstead. (SEP., ANT., *and* HALL *disappear. Noise without*).

PODDLES (*without*).—Let me pass. My nephew William would not refuse admittance to his uncle Peter. (*Enter. Stands opposite the chair at L., end of table*). Ah, there you are, studying like a good boy. (WILD. *rises*. PODD. *shakes his hand*). How are you? I wish you many happy returns of the day, William. You see I have not forgotten that it was your birthday.

WILD.—Is that you, Uncle Peter?

[HALL. *peeps over the back of the table.*]

PODD.—Why, of course it's me. You did not expect me, I know, but you are glad to see me, arn't you? Why of course you are. (*Puts his umbrella and white hat on the table*. HALL. *puts the hat on the* L *chair*). You are always glad to see your uncle Peter. (*Takes snuff-box from his vest pocket and takes a pinch of snuff*). That servant would not let me in, William; he said you were very busy. You did not want to be interrupted in your studies, I suppose, and quite right, too. What book are you studying now? (*Takes the book from the table fixes his double eye-glass. reads*). The Plundering Pirates' Perfidy, or, the Ragman's Revenge! (*Sternly*). William, what is the meaning of this?

WILD. (*Is embarrassed.   Aside*).—Confound it, that's Moses' book I got hold of! What can I say? (*Aloud*). Well, uncle, I—I er—was not reading the er—Ragman's Revenge! You see I—er was thinking about something else when I took the book up. It isn't mine, uncle; it belongs to that youth whom you saw outside!

PODD.—Oh, indeed; and this is the kind of literature that he reads, is it? Bah! (*Dashes the book on the table.   Sits on his hat*). Bless me! (*Rises quickly, takes his crushed hat from chair*). Why, I have sat on my hat! How very careless of me to be sure; I thought I had put it on the table. (*Puts it on the table L.   Sees the hats belonging to* HALL., ANT., SEP., *and* WILD. *on the table*). William, what extravagance is this? One, two, three, four hats. Tell your uncle Peter what it means?

ANT. (*Looks out.   Aside*).—This is worse than a Turkish bath.

WILD. (*aside*).—Confound it, I forgot to remove them, (*Aloud.*) Oh, the er—hats, uncle? Yes of course, they are er—hats!

PODD.—Precisely, but *four* hats, William.

WILD.—Well er—*perhaps* some of the other lodgers may have er—left one of their spare hats in this room some time or other, and er—

PODD.—You should not allow them to do so, William; it gives the room such a untidy appearance. This is yours, I suppose, with your initials inside. I will throw the others out, and then the lodgers will know better than leave their hats lying about your room. (*Goes to door,* HALL. *raises the tablecloth, seizes* WILD'S *leg.*)

HALL. (*aside to* WILD).—I say Will, don't let him throw my hat away. WILD. *tries to push him under the table with his foot,* SEP. *looks out.*)

SEP. (*Aside to* WILD),—Stop him, Will, I can't go home without my hat, you know.

ANT. (*aside to* WILD).—Hist! William, save my hat; it is the only one I have. (WILD *is bewildered, makes signs to them all to be quiet.* PODD. *is looking out at the door.*)

PODD.—There's one (*throws a hat out*). There's two (*throws another out*). There's three (*throws another out.   Calls*)—Hi, boy! you can take those hats to the marine stores and sell them.

HALL., SEP., ANT.—Marine stores. (*They disappear*).

PODD. (*Comes to front*).—Yes, the marine stores, William. (*Sits L end of table, takes a pinch of snuff.* WILD. *sits* R). I suppose my arrival here was quite a pleasant surprise, William, was it not?

WILD.—It was quite unexpected, uncle, I can assure you.

PODD.—I've no doubt it was. I have been transacting a little business, and calling on my old friends, or I should have been here earlier.

HALL. (*looks out*).—Don't apologise; you are quite soon enough. (*Knock at door*).

WILD.—Come in.

MOSES (*Enters*).—Mrs. Moppy says the banquet is ready, and will you and the other gentlemen come to the dining-room immediately.

PODD.—Banquet!—gentlemen! William, what does this mean?

WILD. (*aside*).—Confound it, fate is against me. (*Aloud*). Banquet, Moses! There is something wrong. Oh, by the way, I heard Mr. Rogers, the second floor lodger, speaking about a banquet the other day. You had better see him, Moses.

MOSES.—All right, sir. (*Aside*). Where's the other gentlemen gone? Things look *very* wrong, don't they, Moses?—oh, rawther. (*Exit*.)

PODD.—I'll go bail that the gentleman who ordered the banquet does not earn his money by the sweat of his brow. His father, or uncle, or some other rich relative, provides him with it, and therefore the expense does not trouble him. Banquet, indeed! Bah! I am very glad that you don't indulge in extravagance of this kind, William—very glad indeed. (*Takes a pinch of snuff. Knock at door. Enter Mrs. MOPPY; she appears excited.*)

Mrs. M.—What's this you say about the bank-et, Mr. Wildair?

WILD. (*Rises hastily. Aside to her*).—It's all right; it's only my joking. I'll be down presently, Mrs. Moppy. Don't let this gentleman hear you. (*Pushing her gently towards the door*).

Mrs. M.—It's past five o'clock, an' the things will all spile if you don't come at onct. (*Exit*.)

PODD.—William, are you deceiving your uncle Peter?

WILD.—Do you think I would do so, uncle Peter?

PODD.—Forgive me, William; your uncle Peter was wrong. By the bye I am going to stay with you a few days, William. I want to see what progress you have made in your studies.

WILD. (*aside*).—I am in for it, now. (*Aloud*.) Studies, did you say, uncle? Ah, yes, to be sure! you said you would come some time.

MOSES (*knocks and enters*).—Mrs. Moppy says the ducks are drying to cinders.

WILD.—And what is that to me? Confound the ducks!

Moses.—We can't sir ; they are *roasted.* (*Exit.*)

Podd.—William, I think you are concealing something from your uncle Peter.

Sep. (*Looks out.* *Aside*).—He is ; he has concealed three of us.

Wild.—What have I to conceal, uncle ? You know——

Moses. (*knocks and enters.*)—Please sir, Mrs. Moppy says the taters are going as cold as ice.

Wild.—Avaunt! (Moses *runs out*). Did you ever see such a tiresome individual as that, uncle ? What would you do with him ?

Podd.—Get him discharged, William.

Moses (*peeps in at door*).—Please, sir the salmon is——,

Wild.—Will you go away ? (Moses *disappears.*) He is only doing it to aggravate me, you know.

Podd.—Get him discharged, William. That is what your uncle Peter advises. (*Is taking a pinch of snuff.* Moses *enters.*)

Moses.—Mrs. Moppy says you didn't ought to keep the——

Wild, *rises, throws the book at* Moses. Podd. *jumps off his seat, upsets his snuff box and lets the box fall to the floor.* Moses *runs out.*)

Podd.—Bless me, William, how you startled me. I have upset my snuff box.

Wild.—You have no need to tell me that, uncle. I can—I can ——ah! ah! (*sneezes*). By Jove, uncle, you take very strong snuff. (Sep. *sneezes, then* Hall. *sneezes.*)

Ant. (*looks out—Aside*).—What is the meaning of this snee—snee sneezing!—ah ! ah !—(*sneezes and disappears.* Wild. *is agitated,* Podd. *looks round in astonishment; does not see* Ant.),

Podd.—William, from whence proceed those mysterious sounds of sneezing ?

Wild.—Oh, er—I did not tell you about the er—remarkable echo that this room has, did I ?

Podd.—No, you did not, William. Is there—(Sep. *and* Hall. *s' eeze*). Hello ! this *is* remarkable ; the echo precedes the original sound, and it seems to come from beneath this table.

Wild.—Oh, by-the-bye, I forgot the cat, uncle. Mrs. Moppy's cat is suffering from a severe cold through staying too long on the tiles at night ; and it is always sneezing er—sometimes—when it sneezes, you know.

Podd.—Poor thing ; I will take it downstairs to the fire. (*Is going to raise the tablecloth,* Wild. *pulls him away*)

Wild.—Don't go near it, uncle, or it will bark at you, and then you'll have the er—measles—the hydrophobia—the whooping-cough —the er— (*Aside.*) Oh, what the dickens am I talking about !

Podd.—William—you are deceiving your uncle Peter.

Wild—Now, uncle—

Podd.—Tut, tut! we shall see (*Looks under the table*). Ah! so this is the *cat*, is it? (*Pulls* Hall. *out by his coat tails*). And pray sir, who are you?

Hall.—A member of the society for the prevention of cruelty to animals. I shall summon you for *cat*-ching and dragging me by my tail.

Sep.—Ha, ha, ha! Good.

Wild. (*aside to* Hall.)—Listen to that goose laughing. It's all over with me now. (*Sits.*)

Po:d.—Is that another cat, William? (*Pulls* Sep. *out*). Well, sir, who are you?

Hall,(*aside to* Sep., *behind* Poddles).—Go on, say something.

Sep.—Something!

Podd.—Undoubtedly! you look like something.

Hall.—He's an ass, that's what he is.

Ant. (*gets out of chest*).—As the others are discovered, I may as well reveal myself.

Podd. (*sees* Ant., *starts back in amazement*).—What still another? Are there many more? William, why are these young men concealed in your room?

Wild. (*aside.*)—I shall have to make a clean breast of it; so here go s (*rises*). Uncle Peter, I became acquainted with these young gentlemen some time ago, and this being my birthday, I invited them here to dine with me and spend a jolly evening! but your arrival upset our plans and made it necessary that my guests should submit to an ignominious concealment. You know what followed, and now I await my sentence.

Podd.—It is you then who ordered the banquet to be prepared? I see it all.

Hall.—I don't; but I can smell it.

Podd.—This is tremendous extravagance! William, you have been guilty of a base piece of ingratitude towards your uncle Peter. You have done many things in opposition to his wishes, therefore you must abide by the consequences. I will not intrude any longer, William, but will leave you with your companions. (*Puts his crushed hat on, takes his umbrella*). May I ask where—ah! there it is. (*Takes portmanteau. Sees decanter and glasses.*) What! have you been drinking, too? Shame, William, shame. Did I not always warn you to avoid intoxicating drinks? O, the degeneracy of the youths of this age! But enough of this; I will depart.

From this time forward, William, you and your uncle Peter are strangers. (*Is going out.*)

WILD.—Stay! Hear me before you go.

HALL. (*to* PODDLES).—Yes, of course; take a chair and listen. (PODD. *comes to front,* HALL. *takes his hat off his head,* SEP. *takes his umbrella,* ANT. *takes his portmanteau,* HALL. *places him in a chair.* PODD. *quietly submits*).—Now you look comfortable. Proceed Will.

WILD.—Is it reasonable of you, uncle Peter, after having brought me up in the indulgent manner that you have done, to expect me to forsake my pleasures and give my mind to diligent study all in a moment, as it were? You sent me away from all my friends, and forbade me the acquaintance of any young men in the city. In short, you wished me, who had hitherto led a life of enjoyment, to live in solitude, like a ridiculous hermit or recluse, or something of that sort. Again, I ask, was this reasonable?

(PODDLES *appears to be meditating.*)

ANT.—In my humble opinion I think it is very unreasonable.

HALL.—I consider it unjust in the extreme.

SEP.—I was just going to say the same thing.

ANT. (*to* PODDLES).—Would you be so cruel as to disown your nephew for trying to spend a cheerful hour with his friends? Shakespeare says—

> "With mirth and laughter let old wrinkles come;
> Why should a man, whose blood is warm within,
> Sit like his grandsire cut in alabaster?
> Sleep when he wakes; and creep into the jaundice
> By being peevish?"

Come, do not be unreasonable, Mr. Poddles. "Pray you forget and forgive," as the immortal bard observes.

(*Enter* MOSES *unobserved, picks his book up, and sits reading in a corner.*)

PODD. (*rises*) —Are you, young gentlemen, really anxious that I should pardon my nephew?

SEP., HALL., ANT.—We are.

PODD.—And would you willingly sacrifice one of your pleasures that his pardon might be obtained.

SEP., HALL., ANT.—We would.

PODD.—Then listen. I will forgive my nephew on condition that you and he, from this time forward, shun and abstain from intoxicating drinks of any kind as if they were noxious reptiles that it is our duty to extirpate. Now what do you say?

HALL.—Well er—you must understand that we are not habitual drunkards—far from it—we only take a little in moderation.

PODD.—Bah! I wouldn't give a fig for a moderator. Come, I await your answer. (*The others appear to be conversing together*). What say you? Do you agree to my conditions?

HALL., SEP., ANT.—We do unanimously.

PODD.—William, your hand. (*Shakes hands with* WILDAIR.) You have my forgiveness.

ANT.—"Be blessed for making up this peace." Shakespeare.

PODD. (*Shakes hands with all*).—I am overjoyed at having won a few more over to the temperance cause. I'll take a pinch of snuff. (*Feels in his vest pocket for the box*). No I won't. I haven't got any.

HALL.—Don't mention snuff, please. The thoughts of it's 'nough (snuff) to make me sneeze.

SEP.—Ha, ha, ha! You're at it again.

Mrs. M. (*enters*).—Where is that Moses gone, I wonder? (*Sees him*). What! air yer readin' of that book again?

MOSES.—Ain't I just?—oh, rowther. (*Mrs. MOPPY pursues him round the room. He runs out*).

WILD.—Mrs. Moppy!

Mrs. M.—Sir! Excuge my comin' 'ere him this rude way. Mr. Wildair, but yer knows the cause, and as I——

WILD.—All right, Mrs. Moppy. I want to tell you that we shall be down to dinner directly, so you will oblige by having everything ready.

Mrs. M.—I is very pleaged to hear it, I is. In fac' I——

WILD.—Certainly, Mrs. Moppy; but don't lose any time. (*Pushes her towards the door, gently. Exit* Mrs. M.). You will join us, uncle, will you not?

PODD.—With the greatest pleasure, William; but shall I be in the way?

WILD.—Not at all, uncle. I really don't think our party would have been complete without you. (*Addressing the audience.*) What say you friends? Has my "Uncle Peter's visit" pleased *you?* There—don't all speak at once. If it has, I shall be happy to see you all at my next "Birthday Party."

———

ABEL HEYWOOD & SON, PRINTERS, OLDHAM STREET, MANCHESTER.

www.ingramcontent.com/pod-product-compliance
Lightning Source LLC
Chambersburg PA
CBHW031200090426
42738CB00008B/1410